THE WISDOM
of CONFUCIUS

THE WISDOM
of CONFUCIUS

LONDON: GAY AND HANCOCK, Ltd.
12 & 13 HENRIETTA ST., COVENT GARDEN
1909

Introduction

CONFUCIUS was one of the most illustrious thinkers whose names have been inscribed upon the scroll of antiquity. His birth, it is said, took place about 551 B.C., in China. Nineteen years afterwards he married, having obtained an appointment in connection with the public stores of herds and grain, and later, in his twenty-second year, he commenced his career as a teacher.

Shortly after this the state of Lû falling into confusion, Confucius fled to Ch'î, where he remained for a time. Subsequently, however, he returned to his native state. Till he was fifty years old he lived in comparative retirement, holding no public office; but in 501 B.C. he was appointed Governor of Chung Tû. So conspicuously successful was his administration that he speedily became the trusted adviser of the Duke Ting, and held, first the position of Minister of Works, and then that of Minister of Crimes. Nor was his popularity among the people any less remarkable.

This satisfactory state of affairs was, however, destined to prove of but brief duration. Jealousy and fear between rival states soon broke out, and brought his public career to an untimely conclusion; and having abandoned his ministry, he was forced to lead a life of wandering and exile.

But in spite of these calamities which befel him, the sage, true philosopher that he was, remained true to his principles; and it was during the closing years of his life that he devoted himself especially to the pursuits of literature and music. His death occurred in 497 B.C.

R. DIMSDALE STOCKER.

Contents

vii

The Wisdom
of Confucius

On Government

ACCORDING to the nature of man, government is the greatest thing for him.

WHEN right principles prevail in the empire, there will be no discussion among the common people.

To govern means to make right. If you lead the people uprightly, who will dare not to be upright?

EMPLOY the upright and put aside all the crooked; in this way the crooked can be made to be upright.

Go before the people with your example, and spare yourself not in their affairs.

3

THERE is good government when those who are near are made happy, and when those who are afar are attracted.

THE art of government is to keep its affairs before the mind without weariness, and to attend to them with undeviating consistency.

THERE is government when the prince is prince, the minister is minister ; when the father is father, and the son is son.

IN hearing litigations I am like any other body. What is necessary is to have no litigations.

THE rude tribes of the East and North have their princes, and are not like the States of our great land, which are without them. What is called a great minister is one who serves his ruler according to what is right, and when he finds he cannot do so retires.

HE who exercises government by means of his virtue may be compared to the polar star, which keeps its place, and all the stars turn toward it.

IT is necessary that there should be sufficiency of good, sufficiency of military equipment, and the confidence of the people in their ruler.

WITH the right men the growth of government is rapid, just as the growth of vegetation is rapid. Government is like an easily growing rush.

DIGNITIES should not be conferred on men of evil practices. If they be, how can the people set themselves to correct their ways?

WHEN a country is well governed, poverty and a mean condition are something to be ashamed of. When a country is ill governed, riches and honours are something to be ashamed of.

IN the service of a ruler, a minister should not descend to subjects beneath him, nor set a high value on speeches, nor accept an introduction from improper individuals.

TRULY straightforward was the historiographer Yu. When good government prevailed in his State, he was like an arrow. When bad government prevailed, he was like an arrow.

IF a minister is correct in his own conduct, what difficulty will he have in aiding the government? If he cannot make himself upright, what has he to do with making others upright?

KE K'ANG, distressed about the number of thieves, asked advice of Confucius. Confucius said, "If you, sir, were not covetous, al-

6

though you should reward them to do it, they would not steal."

A MINISTER, in serving his prince, reverently discharges his duties, and makes his emolument a secondary consideration.

WHEN a prince's personal conduct is correct, his government is effective without the issuing of orders. If his personal conduct is not correct, he may issue orders, but they will not be obeyed.

WHEN those who are in high stations perform well all their duties to their relations, the people are aroused to virtue. When old ministers and friends are not neglected by them, the people are preserved from meanness.

WHEN good government prevails in a State, language may be lofty and bold, and actions the same. When bad government prevails, the actions may be lofty and bold, but the language should be with some reserve.

A SUPERIOR man, indeed, is Keu Pih-yuh. When good government prevails in his State, he is to be found in office. When bad government prevails, he can roll his principles up and keep them in his breast.

CHUNG-KUNG, being chief minister to the head of the Ke family, asked about government. The Master said, "Employ first the services of your various officers, pardon small faults, and raise to office men of virtue and talents."

IF good men were to govern a country a hundred years, they would be able to transform the violently bad, and dispense with capital punishments.

TSZE-KUNG asked, "What qualities must a man possess to entitle him to become an officer?" The

Master said, "He who in his conduct preserves a sense of shame, and when sent to any quarter will not disgrace his prince's commission, deserves to be called an officer."

To see men of worth and not be able to raise them to office ; to raise them to office and not be able to do so quickly,—this is treating them with disrespect. To see bad men and not be able to remove them ; to remove them, but not to send them far away,—this is weakness.

Though a man be able to recite the three hundred odes, yet if, when entrusted with governmental commission, he knows not how to act, or if, when sent to any quarter on a mission, he cannot give of himself the proper replies, notwithstanding his attainments, of what practical use are they?

9

Tsze-hae, being governor of Keu-fou, asked about government. The Master said, "Do not be desirous to have things done quickly; do not look at small advantages. Desire to have things done quickly prevents their being done thoroughly. Looking at small advantages prevents great affairs from being accomplished."

To be fond of learning is near to wisdom; to practise with vigour is near to benevolence; to be conscious of shame is near to fortitude. He who knows these three things knows how to cultivate his own character. Knowing how to cultivate his own character, he knows how to govern other men. Knowing how to govern other men, he knows how to govern the kingdom, with its States and families.

A MINISTER in the service of his
ruler will first offer words of
counsel, and when they are
accepted, he will bow and volun-
tarily offer his person to make
good his sincerity. Hence, whatever services a ruler requires
from his minister, the minister
will die in support of his words.
In this way the salary he receives
is not obtained on false pre-
tences, and the things for which
he may be blamed will be fewer
and fewer.

THE exemption of nobles and high
dignitaries from the application
of the penal laws was based upon
the assumption that men destined
to occupy such honourable and
prominent positions would be
found superior to the faults and
failings of those who had not en-
joyed the advantages of fortune.
That exemption has been made
from a desire to place the ruling

classes before the public in such a light as would cause them to be regarded with special veneration.

THE king's words are at first as threads of silk ; but when sent forth they become as cords. Or, they are at first as cords, but when sent forth they become as ropes. Therefore, the great man does not lead in idle speaking. The superior man does not speak words which may not be embodied in deeds, nor does he actions which may not be expressed in words. When this is the case, the words of the people may be carried into action without risk, and their actions can be spoken of without risk.

IN passing by the side of Mount Thai, Confucius came on a woman who was weeping bitterly by a grave. The Master pressed forward and drove quickly to her; then he sent Tze-lu to question her. "Your wailing," said he, "is that of one who has suffered sorrow on sorrow." She replied, "That is so. Once my husband's father was killed here by a tiger. My husband was also killed, and now my son has died in the same way." The Master said, "Why do you not leave the place?" The answer was, "There is no oppressive government here." The Master then said, "Remember this, my children: oppressive government is more terrible than tigers."

THE kings of three dynasties, in taking care of the old, always had the ages of those connected with them brought to their notice. At eighty a son was free from all government service. At ninety all the members of the family were released from government duty. In the case of those who were disabled or ill, and required attendance, one man was discharged from those duties. Those mourning for their parents had a discharge for three years. Those mourning for a year or nine months had a discharge for three months.

Orphans, an old man without sons, an old man who has lost his wife, and an old woman who has lost her husband ; these four were considered as the most forlorn of heaven's people, for they had none to whom they could tell their wants. These all received regular allowances.

· · · The feast on grain-fed animals accompanied by drinking was not intended to have bad effects ; yet cases of litigation are more numerous in consequence of it. It is the excessive drinking which produces the evil.

Therefore the old kings framed rules to regulate drinking. Where there is but one presentation of the cup at one time, guest and host may bow to each other a hundred times without getting drunk. This was the way in which those kings guarded against this evil.

THERE were five things by which the ancient kings secured the good government of the whole kingdom, — the honour which they paid to the virtuous, to the noble and to the old, the reverence they paid to the aged, and their kindness to the young. It was by these five things that they maintained the stability of the kingdom.

On Doctrine

HEAVEN produced the virtue that is in me.

SIN, my doctrine is that of an all-pervading unity.

WHILE you do not know about life, how can you know about death?

THE great attribute of heaven and earth is the giving and maintaining of life.

WHILE you are not able to serve men, how can you serve their spirits?

WITHOUT recognizing the ordinances of Heaven it is impossible to be a superior man.

How abundantly do spiritual beings display the powers that belong to them!

We look for them, but do not see them; we listen, too, but do

not hear them ; yet they enter
into all things, and there is nothing without them.

IN dealing with the dead, if we treat
them as if they were entirely
dead, that would show a want
of affection, and should not be
done ; or, if we treat them as if
they were entirely alive, that
would show a want of wisdom,
and should not be done.

HEAVEN overspreads all without partiality.   Earth sustains all without partiality.   The sun and
moon shine on all without partiality.   Reverently displaying
these three characteristics, and
thereby comforting, under the
toils which they impose, all under
heaven, is what is called " The
Three Impartialities."

HEAVEN and earth existing, all things
got their existence.   All things

having existence, afterwards there came male and female. From the existence of male and female there came afterwards husband and wife. From husband and wife there came father and son. From father and son there came minister and ruler. From ruler and minister there came high and low. When high and low had existence, afterwards came the arrangements of propriety and righteousness.

THE sage, looking up, contemplates the brilliant phenomena of the heavens, and, looking down, examines the definite arrangements of the earth. Thus he knows the causes of darkness and light. He traces things from their beginning and follows them to their end. Thus he knows what can be said of death and life. He perceives how the union of essence and breath forms things, and the

18

flight of the soul produces the change in their constitution. Thus he knows the characteristics of the anima and the animus.

When we speak of spirit we mean the subtle presence of God with all things. For putting things in motion there is nothing more vehement than thunder; for scattering them there is nothing more effective than wind; for drying there is nothing more parching than fire; for giving them satisfaction there is nothing more grateful than a lake or marsh; for moistening them there is nothing more enriching than water; for bringing them to an end and then giving them fresh impetus there is nothing more completely adapted than *Kan*. Thus water and fire assist one another; thunder and wind do not act contrary to each other; mountains and collections of water interchange their influences. It is in this way that these are able to change and transform, and to give completion to all things.

On Ethics

WHAT you do not like when done to yourself, do not do to others.

To fell a single tree, to kill a single animal, not at the proper season, is contrary to filial piety.

MAN is born for uprightness. If a man lose his uprightness and yet live, his escape from death is mere good fortune.

ARDENT, yet not upright; stupid, and yet not attentive; simple, and yet not sincere,—such persons I do not understand.

IN the Book of Poetry are three hundred pieces, but the design of all may be embraced in the one phrase, — "Have no depraved thoughts."

21

HOLD faithfulness and sincerity as first principles. Have no friends not equal to yourself. When you have faults, do not fear to abandon them.

THERE are three thousand offences, against which the five punishments are directed, and there is not one of them greater than being unfilial.

HAVING not, yet affecting to have; empty, yet affecting to be full; straitened, yet affecting to be in easy circumstances, — it is difficult with such characteristics to be consistent.

TSZE-KUNG asked, "Is there one word which may serve as a rule of practice for all one's life?" The Master said, "Is not reciprocity such a word? What you do not want done to yourself, do not do to others."

Tsze-loo then said, "I should

like, sir, to hear your wishes."
The Master said, "In regard to
the aged, to give them rest; in
regard to friends, to show them
sincerity; in regard to the young,
to treat them tenderly."

SOME one said, "What do you say
concerning the principle that injury should be returned with
kindness?" The Master said,
"With what, then, will you
recompense kindness? Recompense injury with justice, and
recompense kindness with kindness."

SINCERITY is the way of heaven.
The acquirement of sincerity belongs to man. He who is sincere hits what is right, and
apprehends without the exercise
of thought. He is the sage who
naturally and easily follows the
right course. He who attains to
sincerity is he who chooses what
is good, and firmly holds it fast.

To lie under arms and meet death without regret — this is the strength of Northern regions, and the strong make it their study.

To show forbearance and gentleness in teaching others, and not revenge unreasonable conduct, this is the strength of Southern regions, and the good man makes it his study.

HARD is the case of him who will stuff himself with food the whole day without applying his mind to anything. Are there not gamesters and chess-players? To be one of these would be still better than doing nothing at all.

LET a man who is ignorant be fond of using his own judgment; let one who is in a low situation be fond of arrogating the directing of things; let one who is in the present age go back to the ways of antiquity—on all such, calamity is sure to come.

It cannot be when the root is neglected that what should spring from it will be well ordered. It never has been the case that what was of great importance has been slightly cared for, and, at the same time, that what was of slight importance has been greatly cared for.

Humanity is like a heavy vessel, and like a long road. He who tries to lift the vessel cannot sustain its weight; he who travels the road cannot accomplish all its distance. There is nothing that has so many different degrees as humanity; and thus who tries to nerve himself to compass it finds it a difficult task.

If a man be under the influence of anger his conduct will not be correct. The same will be the case if he be under the influence of terror, or of fond regard, or of sorrow, or distress. When the mind is not present, we look, but we do not see; we hear, and we do not understand; we eat, and we do not know the taste of what we eat. This is what is meant by saying the cultivation of the individual depends on the right education of the mind.

If acts of goodness be not accumulated, they are not sufficient to give its stamp to one's reputation. If acts of evil be not accumulated, they are not sufficient to destroy one's reputation. The small man thinks that small acts of goodness are of no benefit, and does not do them; and that small deeds of evil do no harm, and does not refrain from them. Hence, his wickedness becomes so great that it cannot be concealed, and his guilt so great that it cannot be pardoned.

WISDOM, benevolence, and fortitude —these three are the universal virtues. The means by which they are practised is another thing. Some are born with a knowledge of these duties ; some know them by study ; some gain them as the result of painful experience. But the knowledge being possessed, it comes to one and the same thing. Some practise them with the ease of nature ; some for the sake of their advantage ; and some by dint of great effort. But when the work of them is done, it comes to one and the same thing.

THE duties of universal obligation are five, and the virtues wherewith they are practised are three. The duties are those between sovereign and minister, between

father and son, between elder
brother and younger, and those
belonging to the intercourse of
friends. Those five are the duties
of universal obligation. Knowledge, magnanimity, and energy;
these three are the virtues uni-
versally binding, and the means
by which they carry these obli-
gations into practice is singleness
of purpose.

MEN are partial where they feel affection and love ; partial where they
despise and dislike ; partial where
they stand in awe, and entertain
feelings of respect ; partial where
they feel sorrow and compassion ;
partial where they are arrogant
and rude. Thus it is that there
are few men in the world who
love, and at the same time know
the bad qualities of the object of
their love, or hate, and yet know
the good qualities of the object
of their hatred. Hence, we have

the common adage: "A man
does not know the badness of his
son; he does not know the rich-
ness of his growing corn."

On Virtue

I HAVE not seen one who loves virtue as he loves beauty.

THE firm, the enduring, the simple and the modest are near to virtue.

IT is only the truly virtuous man who can love or can hate others.

Is virtue a thing remote ? I wish to be virtuous, and lo, virtue is at hand.

FINE words and an insinuating appearance are seldom associated with virtue.

THE doings of the Supreme Heaven have neither sound nor smell. That is perfect virtue.

VIRTUE is not left to stand alone. He who practises it will have neighbours.

On Virtue

THERE is Houy. He has nearly attained to perfect virtue. He is often in want.

Is he not a man of perfect virtue who feels no discomposure though men may take no note of him?

Is any one able for one day to apply his strength to virtue? I have not seen the case in which his strength would be insufficient.

SUPERIOR men, yet not always virtuous, there have been. Alas! But there has never been a mean man, and—virtuous.

Now, the man of perfect virtue, wishing to be established himself, seeks also to establish others; wishing to be enlarged himself, he seeks also to enlarge others.

VIRTUE small and office high; wisdom small and plans great; strength small and burden heavy; where such conditions exist, it is seldom that they do not come to naught.

THE virtuous will be sure to speak uprightly ; but those whose speech is all right may not be virtuous. Men of principle are sure to be bold ; but those who are bold may not always be men of principle.

THE Duke of Ts'e had a thousand teams, each of four horses, but on the day of his death the people did not praise him for a single virtue. P'ih-e and Shuh-ts'e died of hunger at the foot of Showyang mountain, and the people down to the present time praise them.

VIRTUE is more to a man than either water or fire. I have seen men die from treading on water and fire, but I have never seen a man die from treading the course of virtue.

FAN-CH'E asked about perfect virtue. The Master said " It is in retirement to be sedately grave; in the management of business to be reverently attentive; in intercourse with others to be strictly sincere. Though a man go among rude, uncultivated tribes, these qualities may not be neglected."

CHUNG-KUNG asked about perfect virtue. The Master said, "It is when you go about to behave to every one as if you were receiving a great guest; to employ the people as if you were assisting at a sacrifice; not to do to others as you would not wish done to yourself; to have no murmuring against you from the public, and none in the family."

HE who aims to be a man of complete virtue, does not seek in his food to gratify his appetite, nor in his dwelling-place does he seek his ease; he is in earnest in what he is doing, and careful in his speech;

he frequents the company of men of principle that he may be kept upright. Such a person may be said indeed to love to learn.

THE ancients who wished to illustrate virtue throughout the Empire, first ordered well their own States. Wishing to order well their States, they first regulated their families. Wishing to regulate their families, they first cultivated their persons. Wishing to cultivate their persons, they first made their hearts right. Wishing to regulate their hearts, they first sought to be sincere in their thoughts. Wishing to be sincere in their thoughts, they first extended to the utmost their knowledge. Such extension of knowledge lay in the investigation of things.

Things being investigated, knowledge became complete. Their knowledge being complete, their thoughts were sincere. Their thoughts being sincere their hearts were then made right. Their hearts being made right, their persons were cultivated. Their persons being cultivated, their families were regulated. Their families being regulated, their States were rightly governed. Their States being well governed, the whole Empire was made tranquil and happy.

On Learning

THERE being instruction, there will be no distinction of classes.

WITHOUT knowing the force of words it is impossible to know men.

IN language it is simply required to convey the meaning.

IT is not possible for one to teach others who cannot teach his own family.

LEARNING without thought is labour lost ; thought without learning is perilous.

Is it not pleasant to learn with unfailing perseverance and application?

LEARN as if you could not reach your object, and also feared lest you should lose it.

On Learning

THE scholar who cherishes a love of comfort is not fit to be deemed a scholar.

IF the scholar be not grave, he will not call forth any veneration, and his learning will not be solid.

A SCHOLAR whose mind is set on truth and who is ashamed of his bad clothes and bad food, is not fit to talk to.

I HAVE been the whole day without eating and the whole night without sleeping, — occupied with thinking. It was no use. The better plan is to learn.

WHEN I walk along with two others, they may prove to be my teachers. I will select their good qualities, and follow them ; their bad qualities, and avoid them.

IF names be not correct, language is not in accordance with the truth of things. If language be not in accordance with the truth of things, affairs cannot be carried to success.

"Yew, shall I teach you what knowledge is? When you know a thing, to hold that you know it; and when you do not know a thing, to allow that you do not know it. This is knowledge."

There are two among his subjects that the ruler does not treat as his subjects. When one is personating his ancestor he does not treat him as a subject, nor does he so treat his Master.

If another man succeed by one effort, he will use a hundred. If another succeed by ten, he will use a thousand. Let a man proceed in this way, and, though stupid, he is sure to become intelligent; though weak, he is sure to become strong.

38

On Learning

When a man of talents and virtue knows the difficulty and the ease in acquiring learning, and knows the good and the bad qualities of learning, he can vary his methods of teaching. When he can vary his methods of teaching, he can be a Master indeed.

I do not open up the truth to any one who is not eager, nor help any one who is not anxious to help himself. When I have presented one corner of a subject to any one, and he cannot from it learn the other three, I do not repeat my lesson.

The master who skilfully waits to be questioned may be compared to a bell when it is struck. Struck with a small hammer, it gives a small sound; struck with a great one, it gives a great sound. But let it be struck leisurely and properly, and it gives out all the sound of which it is capable.

THERE are some with whom we may study in common, but we shall find them unable to go along with us to principles. We may go on with them to principles, but we will find them unable to get fixed in those principles. Or, if we get fixed in those principles with them, we will find them unable to weigh occurring events along with us.

LEARNING may be compared to what happens in raising a mound. If there be wanting but one basketful to complete the mound and I stop, the stopping is my own work. It may be compared to levelling a mound. Though but one basketful is thrown off at a time, the progress is my own going forward.

THE rules aimed at in the Great College were the prevention of evil before it was manifested; the timeliness of instruction just when it was required ; the suitability of the lessons in adaptation to circumstances ; and the good influence of example to all those concerned. It was from these four things that the teaching was so flourishing.

THE ancients in prosecuting their learning compared different things and traced the analogies between them. The drum has no special relation to any of the musical notes, but without it they cannot be harmonized. Water has no particular relation to any of the five colours, but without it they cannot be displayed. Learning has no particular relation to any of the five senses, but without it they cannot be regulated.

THE scholar does not consider gold and jade to be precious treasures, but loyalty and good faith. He does not desire lands and territory, but considers the establishment of righteousness his domain. He does not desire a great accumulation of wealth, but looks on many accomplishments as his riches. It is difficult to win him, but easy to pay him. It is easy to pay him, but difficult to retain him.

To be fond of learning is to be near to knowledge. To act with vigour is to be near to magnanimity. To possess the feeling of shame is to be near to energy.

He who knows these three things knows how to cultivate his own character. Knowing how to cultivate his own character, he knows how to govern other men. Knowing how to govern other men, he knows how to govern the Empire with all its States and families.

WITH the scholar friendly relations may be cultivated, but no attempt must be made to restrain him. Near associations with him may be sought, but cannot be forced upon him. He may be killed, but he cannot be disgraced. In his dwelling he will not be extravagant. In his eating and drinking he will not be luxurious. He may be gently admonished of his errors and failings, but he should not have them enumerated to his face—such is his boldness and determination.

THE extension of knowledge is by the investigation of things. Things being investigated, the knowledge of them becomes complete. Knowledge being complete, the thoughts were sincere. The thoughts being sincere, the hearts were made upright. The hearts being upright, the person was cultivated. The person being cultivated, families were regulated. Families being regulated, the

States were rightly governed. The States being rightly governed, the whole kingdom was made tranquil and happy.

PROHIBITION of evil after it has been manifested meets with opposition, and cannot be carried out successfully. Instruction given after the time for it is past is done with toil and prosecuted with difficulty. Giving lessons in an undiscriminating manner, and with lack of fitness, causes injury and disorder, and fails in its object. Learning alone and without companions makes one feel solitary, rude, and without intelligence. Friendships of festal occasions lead to opposition to one's Master. Friendships with the dissolute lead to the neglect of one's learning.

THE scholar recommends members of his own family to public

employment without hesitation, because of their kinship, and proposes others without regard to their enmity to him. He estimates men's merits, and takes into consideration all their services, selecting those of virtue and ability, putting them forward without expecting any recompense from them. The ruler thus gets what he wishes, and if benefit results to the State, the scholar does not seek riches or honours for himself. Such is his place in promoting the employment of the worthy and bringing forward the able.

THE scholar will not take the high office of minister to the Son of Heaven, nor the low office of serving a prince of a State. He is watchful of himself in retirement, and values a generous enlargement of mind; and at the same time is bold and resolute in

45

his intercourse with others. He learns extensively that he may know what should be done; he makes himself acquainted with elegant accomplishments, and thus smooths off all his corners and angles. Although the offer were made to share a State with him, it would be no more to him than the small weights of a balance. He will not take a ministry, he will not take an office. Such are the rules and conduct he prescribes for himself.

THE Six Becloudings: There is the love of being benevolent without the love of learning. The beclouding here leads to foolish simplicity. There is the love of knowing without the love of learning. The beclouding here leads to an injurious disregard of consequences. There is the love of straightforwardness without the love of learning. The beclouding here leads to rudeness. There is the love of boldness without the love of learning. The beclouding here leads to insubordination. There is the love of firmness without the love of learning. The beclouding here leads to extravagant conduct.

On Marriage

CEREMONIES are the first thing to be attended to in the practice of government. Yes, the ceremony of marriage lies at the foundation of government.

WITH the ancients in their practice of government, the love of men was the great point. In their regulation of the love of men, the rules of ceremony was the great point. In their regulation of those rules, reverence was the great point. For the extreme manifestation of reverence, we find the best illustration in the great rite of marriage.

THE ceremony of marriage was intended to be a bond of love between families of two different surnames, with a view in its retrospective character to maintaining the services in the ancestral temple ; and in its prospective character, to secure the continuance of the family line. Therefore the greatest men, the ancient rulers, set a great value upon it.

HENCE in regard to the various introductory ceremonies : the proposal with its accompanying gift, the inquiries about the lady's name, the notice of the approving divination, receiving the special offerings, and the request to fix the day—these all were received by the principal party on the lady's side, as he was seated on the mat or leaning stool in the ancestral temple.

WHEN they arrived, he met the messenger and greeted him outside the gate, giving place to him as he entered ; after which they ascended to the hall. Thus were the instructions received in the ancestral temple, and in this way the ceremony was respected, and watched over, and its importance was shown and care taken that all its details should be correct.

THE respect, the caution, the importance, the attention to secure correctness in all the details—and then mutual affection. These were the great points of the ceremony, and served to establish the distinction to be observed between man and woman, and the righteousness to be maintained between husband and wife. From the distinction between man and woman came the righteousness between husband and wife; from that righteousness came the affection between father and son; and from that affection the right feeling between ruler and minister. Whence it is said, "The ceremony of marriage is at the root of the other ceremonial observances."

50

THEREFORE, formerly the young lady, for three months before her marriage, was taught in the high temple of the ancestor of her surname, if it was still standing, as befitting the public hall of the members of her surname. If it were no longer standing she was taught in the public hall of the head of that branch of the surname to which she belonged. She was taught there the virtue, the speech, the carriage, and the work of a wife. When the teaching was over, she offered sacrifice to the ancestor, using fish for the victim, and soups made of duckweed and pondweed. So was she trained to the obedience of a wife.

A SPECIAL apartment was prepared in the palace for the child, and from all the concubines and other proper persons there was sought one distinguished for her generosity of mind, her gentle kindness, her

mild integrity, her respectful bearing, her carefulness and freedom
from talkativeness, who should
be appointed the boy's teacher.
One was next chosen who should
be his indulgent mother, and a
third who should be his guardian
mother. These all lived in his
apartment, which others did not
enter, unless on business.

FORMERLY the queen of the Son of
Heaven divided the harem into
six palace halls, occupied by three
ladies called the fu-zan, nine called
the pin, twenty-seven the shih-fu,
and eighty-one the yu-khi. These
were instructed in the domestic
and private rule which should
prevail throughout the kingdom,
and how the deferential obedience
of the wife should be illustrated.
Thus internal harmony was everywhere secured and families regulated. In the same manner, the
Son of Heaven appointed six

official departments, in which were distributed the three kung, the nine khing, the twenty - seven ta-fu, and the eighty-one sze of the highest grade. These were instructed in all that concerned the public and external government of the kingdom, and how the duties of the man should be illustrated. Thus harmony was secured in all external affairs, and the States were properly governed.

On Family Relations

FILIAL piety is the constant rule of Heaven, the righteousness of earth, and the practical duty of man.

IT is said in the Book of Poetry, "Happy union with wife and children is like the music of lutes and harps. When there is concord among brothers the harmony is delightful and enduring. Thus may you regulate your family and enjoy the pleasure of your wife and children."

HERE now is the affection of a father for his sons: He loves the worthy among them, and places on a level those who do not show ability. But that of a mother for them is such, that while she loves the worthy, she pities those who do not show ability. The mother deals with them through her affections, and is not concerned with showing them honour. The father is intent on showing them honour, and is not concerned with his affections.

FORMERLY the intelligent kings served their fathers with filial piety, and therefore they served Heaven with intelligence. They served their mothers with filial piety, and therefore they served the earth with discrimination. They pursued the right course with their seniors and juniors, and their example established the relation between superiors and inferiors.

OF all that Heaven produces and nourishes, there is none so great as man. His parents give birth to his person all complete, and to return it to them all complete may be called a filial duty. When no member has been mutilated and no disgrace done to any part of the person, it may be called complete. Hence a superior man does not care to take the slightest step in forgetting this filial duty. But now I forget the way of that, and therefore I wear the look of sorrow.

THE superior man, while his parents are alive, reverently nourishes them ; and, when they are dead, reverently sacrifices to them. His thought to the end of his life is how not to disgrace them. The saying that a superior man mourns all his life for his parents has reference to the day of their death. That he does not do his ordinary work on that day does not mean that it would be unpropitious to do so ; it means that on that day his thoughts are occupied with them, and he does not dare to occupy himself, as on other days, with his private and personal affairs.

On Family Relations

THE disciple Shan said, " I venture
to ask whether in the virtue of
the sages there was not something
greater than filial piety." The
Master replied, " Of all natures
produced by Heaven and earth,
man is the noblest. Of all the
actions of man there is none
greater than filial piety. In filial
piety there is nothing greater than
the reverential awe of one's father.
In the reverential awe of one's
father there is nothing greater
than in making him the correlate
of Heaven."

Now the feeling of affection grows up
at the parents' knees, and as
nourishing those parents is practised, the affection daily merges
into awe. The sages proceeded
from this awe to teach reverence,
and from affection to teach love.
The teaching of the sages, without
being severe, was successful ; and
their government, without being

rigorous, was effective. What they proceeded from was the root.

THE ancient kings, seeing how their teachings could transform the people, set before them, therefore, the example of the most all-embracing love, and none of the people neglected their parents. They set forth to them virtue and righteousness, and the people roused themselves to the practice of these. They went before the people with reverence and courtesy, and the people had no quarrels. They led them on by the rules of propriety and by music, and the people were harmonious and benignant. They showed them what they loved and what they disliked, and the people understood their desires and prohibitions.

On Duties of Sons

A BOY should never be allowed to see an instance of deceit.

A LAD should not wear a jacket of fur or the skirt. He must stand straight and square, and not incline his head in hearing.

IT is the rule for all sons that in the winter they should warm the bed for their parents, and to cool it in summer; in the evening to make everything ready, and to make inquiries in the morning. When with their companions they must not quarrel.

WHEN an older person is holding a boy by the hand, the boy should hold the elder's hand with both hands. When the elder has shifted his sword to the back and is speaking to him with his face bent down, the boy should cover his mouth with his hand in answering.

When following one older they ascend to a level, he must keep his face toward the quarter to which the older is looking. When he has climbed to the wall of a city, he should not point or call out. When he goes to a lodging house, let it not be with the feeling he must get whatever he asks for.

When he is following his teacher, he should not quit the road to speak to another person. When he meets his teacher on the road, he should hasten to him and stand with his hands joined across the breast. If the teacher speak to him, he will answer ; if he do not, he will retire with hasty steps.

A son when he is going away must let it be known ; when he returns, he must present himself before his parents. The region in which he travels must be well known ; and he must engage in some occupation.

WHILE his parents are alive, a son should not dare to consider his wealth his own ; nor to hold any of it for his private use.

WHEN he sees an intimate friend of his father, he must not go toward him without being invited to do so ; nor to withdraw without being told ; nor to address him without being questioned. This is the conduct of a filial son.

A YOUTH is to be regarded with respect. How do we know that his future will not be equal to our present ? If he reach the age of forty or fifty, and has not made himself heard of, then he will indeed not be worthy of respect.

IN serving his parents, a son may remonstrate with them, but gently. When he sees that they do not follow his advice, he should show an increased reverence, but not abandon his purpose. Should they punish him, he must not allow himself to murmur.

IN ordinary conversation he should not use the term "old." He should serve one twice as old as himself as he serves his father; one ten years older than himself as an elder brother; with one five years older, he should walk shoulder to shoulder, but behind him. When five are sitting together, the eldest should have a different mat.

IF the door is open, he should leave it open; if it was shut, he must shut it again. If there are others to enter after him, he must not shut it hastily. Let him not tread

62

on the shoes, not stride across the mat ; but let him hold up his dress and move quickly to his corner. He must be careful in answering and assenting.

On going up to the hall he must raise his voice. When outside a door, if there be two shoes and voices are heard, he may enter; if voices be not heard, he must not enter. On entering a door he must keep his eyes cast down. As he enters he should keep his hands raised, as if bearing the bar of the door. In looking up or down, he should not turn.

He should not ascend a height, nor approach the edge of a precipice. He should not indulge in reckless reviling or in derisive laughter. A filial son will not do things in the dark, nor attempt dangerous undertakings, lest he disgrace his parents. While his parents are,

alive he will not promise a friend
to die, nor will he have wealth
that he calls his own.

" ALTHOUGH your father and mother
are dead, if you propose to yourself any good work, only reflect
how it will make their names illustrious, and your purpose will be
fixed. So if you propose to do
what is not good, only consider
how it will disgrace the name of
your father, and you will desist
from your purpose."

A SON should not occupy the south-
west corner of the apartment, nor
sit in the middle of the mat, nor
stand in the middle of the door-
way. He should not assume to
determine the rice and other viands
at an entertainment. He should
not act as personator of the dead
at sacrifice. He should be hearing them when there is no sound
from them, and seeing them when
they are not actually there.

On Duties of Sons

THE service which a filial son does
for his parents is as follows : In
his general conduct to them he
manifests the utmost reverence ;
in his care of them his endeavour
is to give them the utmost pleasure ; when they are ill, he feels
the greatest anxiety ; in mourning
for them he shows every demon-
stration of grief ; in sacrificing to
them he displays the utmost
solemnity. When a son is complete in these five things, he is
able to serve his parents.

A son should not forget his parent
in the single lifting up of his feet,
nor in the utterance of a single
word. Therefore he will walk in
the highway and not take a by-
path ; he will use a boat and not
attempt to wade through a stream,
not daring with the body left him
by his parents to put it in peril.
He should not forget his parents
in the utterance of a single word.

E   65

Therefore an evil word will not issue from his mouth, and an angry word will not assail him. Not to disgrace his person, and not to cause shame to his parents, may be called filial piety.

IN serving his father, a son should conceal his faults, and not speak plainly to him about them. He should in every possible way wait on him and nourish him, without being tied to definite rules. He should serve him laboriously till his death, and then complete the three years' mourning for him. In serving his ruler he should remonstrate with him openly and strongly, and make no concealment. He should in every possible way wait on him and nourish him, but according to definite rules. He should serve him laboriously till his death; and should then wear mourning for him according to rule for three years. In serving his teacher, it is not his business to reprove him or comment on his faults. He should in every way wait upon and serve him, without being tied to definite rules, and should serve him untiringly till his death, and mourn for him in heart for three years.

On Women

NO instructions or orders must issue from the harem.

WOMEN's business is simply the preparation and supplying of wine and food.

SHE may take no step of her own motion, and may come to no conclusion in her own mind.

BEYOND the threshold of her apartments she should not be known for evil or for good. She may not cross the boundaries of a State to accompany a funeral.

THERE never has been a girl who learned first to bring up an infant that she might afterwards be married.

IF a mother be really anxious about it, though she may not exactly hit the wants of her infant, she will not be far from it.

WITH the son of a widow one does not have interviews. This would seem to be an obstacle to friendship, but a superior man will refrain from intercourse of this sort to avoid suspicion.

IN driving with a woman one must drive with one hand and keep the other behind his back.

IN the intercourse of friends, if the master of the house be not in, a visitor, unless for some imperative reason, does not enter.

This is intended to preserve the people from evil ; and yet there are those who prefer vanity to virtue.

MAN is the representative of Heaven, and is supreme over all things. Woman yields obedience to the institutions of man, and helps him to carry out his principles. On this account she can determine nothing of herself, and is subject

69

to the rule of the three obedi-
ences. When young, she must
obey her father and elder brother ;
when married, she must obey her
husband ; when her husband is
dead, she must obey her son.
She may not think of marrying
a second time.

WIVES should serve their parents-in-
law as they served their own. At
the first crowing of the cock they
should wash their hands and
rinse their mouths ; comb their
hair and draw over it the cover-
ing of silk, fix this with the hairpin, and tie the hair at the roots
with the fillet. They should then
put on their jacket, and over it
the sash. On the left side they
should hang the duster and hand-
kerchief, the knife and whetstone,
the small spike and the metal
speculum to get fire with. On
the right side they should hang
the needle case, thread and floss,

enclosed in a bag, the great spike and the borer to get fire with from wood. They will also fasten on their necklaces, and tie their shoe strings.

THUS dressed they should go to their parents and parents-in-law. Then with gentle voice and bated breath they should ask if they are warm or cold, if they are ill or suffering, or in any way uncomfortable; and if they be so, they should proceed reverently to stroke and scratch the place. They should also support and help their parents in going or coming, by going before or following after. In bringing the basket for them to wash, the elder will carry the stand, the younger the water. They will beg to be allowed to pour out the water, and when the washing is over, they will hand the towel. They will ask whether they want any-

thing, and will then respectfully
bring it. All this will they do
with an appearance of pleasure
to make their parents feel at ease.
Gruel, thick or thin, spirits or
must, soup with vegetables, beans,
wheat, spinach, rice, millet, maize,
whatever they wish in fact ; with
dates, chestnuts, sugar, and honey
to sweeten their dishes ; also the
ordinary or large-leaved violets,
leaves of the elm-tree, fresh or
dry, and the most soothing rice-
water to lubricate them, and with
fat and oil to enrich them. The
parents will be sure to taste them,
and when they have done so the
young people should withdraw.

On Propriety

EVEN in killing men, observe the rules of propriety.

THERE is nothing better than observance of the rules of propriety for giving security to the upper classes and good government to the people.

FROM the Emperor down to the masses of the people, all must consider the cultivation of the person the root of everything else.

IT is virtuous manners which constitute the excellence of a neighbourhood. If a man in selecting a residence does not fix on one where these prevail, he is not wise.

RESPECT shown without observing the rules of propriety is called vulgarity. Courtesy without observ-

ing these rules, is called forward-
ness. Boldness without observing
them is called violence. Forward-
ness takes away from gentleness
and benevolence.

HUSBAND and wife have separate
functions; between father and son
there should be affection; between
ruler and minister there should
be strict adherence to their several
parts. If these relations be cor-
rectly discharged, all other things
will follow.

RESPECT without the rules of propriety becomes fussiness; carefulness without the rules of propriety
becomes timidity; boldness without the rules of propriety becomes
insubordination ; straightforwardness without the rules of propriety
becomes rudeness.

THE rules of propriety are simply the
principle of reverence. Therefore
the reverence paid to a father

makes the sons pleased. The reverence paid to an elder brother makes younger brothers pleased. The reverence to a ruler makes subjects pleased. The reverence paid to one man makes myriads pleased. This reverence is paid to a few, and the pleasure extends to the many.

COURTESY is near to propriety. Economy is near to humanity. Good faith is near to the truth of things. If these virtues are practised with respect and humility, one may fall into errors, but they will not be very great. Where there is courtesy mistakes are few; where there is truth, there will be good faith; where there is economy the exercise of forbearance is easy. Will not failure be rare in the case of those who practise these things?

WHAT is the object of the rules of ceremony? It is simply the

ordering of affairs. The wise man
who has affairs to attend to must
have a correct way of attending to
them. He who should attempt
to regulate a State without those
rules would be like a blind man
with no one to lead him. Grop-
ing about, how could he find his
way? Or, he would be like one
searching all night in a dark room
without a light. How could he
see anything?

IF a man observes the rules of propriety he is safe; if he do not, he
is in danger. Hence the saying:
the rules of propriety should by
no means be left unlearned. Propriety is seen in humbling one's
self and giving honour to others.
Since porters and peddlers display
this virtue, how much more should
the rich and noble do so! When
the rich and noble come to value
propriety, they do not become
proud or dissolute. When the

poor and mean come to value propriety, they possess mental courage.

On the roads, men took the right side and women the left. A man kept behind another who had a father's years; he followed one who might be his elder brother more closely, but still keeping behind, as geese follow one another in a row. Friends did not pass by one another when going the same way. In bearing burdens, both were borne by the younger; and if the two were too heavy for one, he took the heavier. A man with grey hair was not allowed to carry anything, though he might do it with one hand.

Whoever enters with his guest yields precedence to him at every door. When he reaches the innermost one he begs leave to go in and arrange the seats, and then returns to receive his guest. After the

guest repeatedly declines to enter
he bows to him and goes in. He
passes through the right door,
the guest through the left. He
ascends the eastern, the other the
western steps. If a guest be of
less rank, he must approach the
steps of the host, while the latter
must repeatedly decline this attention. Then the guest may return
to the western steps, he ascending.
Both host and guest must mutu-
ally yield precedence ; then the
host must ascend first, and the
guest follow. From step to step
they must bring their feet together,
gradually ascending — those on
the east moving the right feet
first, those on the west, the left.

In the right government of a State
the rules of propriety serve the
same purpose as the steelyard in
determining what is light and what
is heavy ; or, as the carpenter's
line in determining what is square

and what is round. If the weights
of the steelyard be true, there can
be no imposition in the matter
of weight; if the line be rightly
applied, there will be no doubt
about the evenness of the surface;
if the square and compass be exact,
there will be no uncertainty as to
the shape of the figure. When a
superior man conducts the government of his State with a discrimi-
nating attention to these rules of
propriety he cannot be imposed
on by traitors and impostors.

THE ceremonies of the Court audi-
ences at the different seasons were
intended to illustrate the righteous
relations between ruler and subject; the friendly messages and
inquiries to illustrate the mutual
honour and respect between the
feudal princes; those of mourning
and sacrifice, to illustrate the
kindly feelings of ministers and
sons; those of social meetings in

the country district, to show the order that should prevail between young and old; and those of marriage to exhibit the separation that should be maintained between males and females. Those ceremonies prevent the rise of disorder and confusion, and are like embankments which prevent the overflow of water. He who thinks the old embankments useless, and destroys them, is sure to suffer from the desolation caused by the overflowing water ; and he who considers the old rules of propriety useless, and would abolish them, would be sure to suffer from the calamities of disorder.

IF the ceremonies of marriage were discontinued, the path of husband and wife would be embittered, and there would be many instances of licentiousness and depravity. If the drinking ceremonies at country feasts were discontinued, the order between old and young would be neglected, and quarrelsome litigations would be frequent. If the ceremonies of mourning and sacrifice were omitted, the kindly feeling of officers and sons would be lessened ; there would be a revolt from the observances due to the dead, and forgetfulness of those due to the living. If the ceremonies of friendly messages and court attendances were discontinued, the positions of ruler and subject would be impaired, the conduct of feudal princes be bad, and the ruin wrought by rebellion, encroachment, and oppression would follow.

THEREFORE the instructive and transforming powers of ceremonies are subtle. They stop depravity before it has taken form, causing men to move daily toward what is good, and to keep farther away from that which is evil, without

F 81

being themselves conscious of it. It was on this account that the ancients set so high a value upon them. This sentiment is found in the words of Yi, " The superior man is careful at the beginning ; a mistake then of a hair's breadth will lead to an error of a thousand *li*.

WHAT are the feelings of men ? They are joy, anger, sadness, fear, love, liking, and disliking. These seven feelings do not have to be learned by men. What are the things that men consider right ? Kindness on the part of the father, and filial duty on the part of the son ; gentleness on the part of the elder brother, and obedience on the part of the younger ; righteousness on the part of the husband and submission on the part of the wife ; kindness on the part of elders, and deference on that of juniors ; benevolence on the part of the ruler, and loyalty on that of the minister. These ten are the things which men consider to be right. Truthfulness in speech and the cultivation of amity constitute what are called ' the things valuable to men.' Hence when a sage would regulate the seven feelings of men, and cultivate the ten virtues ; promote truthfulness of speech and the maintenance of amity ; show the worth of kindly consideration and courtesy ; and prevent quarrelling and plundering, if he neglect the rules of propriety, how shall he succeed ?"

On Music

VIRTUE is the strong stem of man's nature, and music is the blossoming of virtue.

WHAT you ask about is music ; what you like is sound. Now music and sound are akin, but they are not the same.

IT was by music that the ancient kings gave elegant expression to their joy. By their armies and axes they gave the same to their anger.

ALL modulations of the voice spring from the minds of men. When the feelings are moved within they are manifested in the sounds of the voice ; and when those sounds are combined so as to form compositions, we have what are called airs.

In music the sages found pleasure, and saw that it could be used to make the hearts of the people good. Because of the deep influence it exerts on a man, and the change it produces in manners and customs, the ancient kings caused it to be one of the subjects of instruction.

Thus the employment of music by the Son of Heaven was intended to reward the most virtuous among the feudal lords. When their virtue was very great and their instructions were honoured, and all the cereals ripened in their season, then they were rewarded by being permitted to have music.

In music, we have the expression of feelings which do not admit of any change ; in ceremonies, that of principles which admit of no alteration. Music embraces what all equally share; ceremonies distinguish the things in which men differ. Hence the theory of music and ceremonies embraces the whole nature of man.

Music carried too far leads to sorrow, and coarseness in ceremonies indicates something awry. To make the grandest music, which should bring with it no element of sorrow, and to frame the completest ceremonies, which could show nothing awry, could be the work only of a great sage.

When the ancient kings had accomplished their undertakings, they made music to commemorate them. When they had established their governments, they framed their ceremonies. The excellence of their music was according to the greatness of their undertakings; and the complete-

ness of their ceremonies was
according to the comprehensive-
ness of their government.

CEREMONIES afforded a clear expression of the people's minds; music
secured the harmonious utterance
of their voices; the laws of government were intended to promote
ceremonies and music, and punishments to guard against their
violation.   When ceremonies,
music, laws, and punishments
had everywhere full sway, without irregularity or collision, the
method of kingly rule was complete.

SIMILARITY and union are the aim
of music; distinction and difference that of ceremony.   From
union comes mutual affection;
from difference, mutual respect.
Where music prevails, we find
weak agreement; where ceremony
prevails, a tendency to separation.

It is the business of these two to blend people's feelings and give elegance to their outward manifestations.

Music comes from within, and ceremonies from without. Music coming from within produces repose of mind; ceremonies coming from without produce elegancies of manner. The highest style of music is sure to be distinguished by ease; the highest style of elegance by its undemonstrativeness.

All modulations of sound take their rise from the mind of man; and music is the intercommunication of them in their relations and differences. Hence even beasts know sound, but not its modulations; and the masses of the people know the modulations, but they do not know music. It is only the superior who can know music.

On Music

MUSIC is the harmony between
Heaven and earth; ceremonies
reflect the orderly distinctions
not the operations of Heaven and
earth. From that harmony all
things receive their being; to
those orderly distinctions they
owe the differences between them.
Music has its origin in Heaven;
ceremonies take their form from
the appearance of earth. If the
imitation of those appearances
were carried to excess, confusion
would appear; if the composition
of music were carried to excess, it
would be too vehement.

WHEN a man is born, he comes as
from Heaven in a state of quiet.
His activity shows itself as he is
acted on by external things, and
develops the desires incident to
his nature. As his perception of
things increases, his knowledge is
increased. Then arise the manifestations of love and hate. When

these are not regulated by anything within, and growing knowledge leads more astray without, he cannot recover himself, and the heavenly principle is lost.

THUS we see that the ancient kings in their institution of ceremonies and music did not seek how fully they could satisfy the desires of the appetite, and of the ears and eyes ; but they intended to teach the people to regulate their likes and dislikes, and to bring them back to the normal course of humanity.

Now there is no end of things by which man is affected ; and when his likes and dislikes are not regulated he is acted upon by external things as they are presented to him. The result is he stifles the voice of the heavenly principle within, and gives indulgence to the desires by which

men may be possessed. Thus
we have the deceitful and rebellious heart, licentious and violent
conduct. The strong press upon
the weak. The many are cruel
to the few. The knowing impose upon the dull. The bold
make it better for the timid. The
diseased are not nursed; the old
and young, the orphans and
lonely are neglected. Such is the
great disorder that ensues.

THEREFORE the ancient kings, when
they instituted their ceremonies
and music, regulated them from
consideration of the requirement
of humanity. By the sackcloth
worn for parents, the wailings and
the weepings, they defined the
terms of the mourning rites. By
the bells, drums, shields, and axes,
they introduced harmony into
their seasons of rest and enjoy-
ment. By marriage, capping, and
the assumption of the hairpin,

they maintained the separation that should exist between male and female. By archery gatherings in the district, and the feasting at the meetings of princes, they provided for the correct maintenance of friendly intercourse.

LET music attain its full results, and there would be no dissatisfied minds ; let ceremony do so, and there would be no quarrels. If courtesies and bowings marked the government of the Kingdom, there would be what might be called music and ceremony indeed. Violent oppression of the people would not take place ; the princes would appear submissively at the court as guest ; there would be no occasion for the weapons of war, and no employment of the five punishments ; the common people would have nothing to complain of, and the Son of Heaven no cause of anger. Such a state of things would be universal music.

IN singing, the high notes rise as if they were borne aloft ; the low descend as if they were falling to the ground. The turns resemble a thing broken off. The finale seems like the breaking of a willow-tree. Emphatic notes are as if they were made by a square. Quavers are like the hooks of a spear. Those prolonged on the same key are like pearls strung together. Hence singing means the prolonged expression of the words. There is the utterance of the words, and when the simple utterance is not sufficient, they prolong expression of them. When the prolonged expression is not enough there comes the sigh and explanation. When these are insufficient, unconsciously comes the motions of the hands and the stamping of the feet.

MUSIC is the production of the modulations of the voice, and its source is in the play of the mind as it is influenced by external things. When the mind is sorrowful, the sound is sharp and loses itself; when it is moved to pleasure, the sound is slow and gentle; when it is moved to joy, the sound is exclamatory and soon disappears; in anger it is coarse and fierce; when the mood is reverential, the sound is frank with a suggestion of humility; when it is moved to love, the sound is harmonious and soft. These six peculiarities of sound are not natural. They indicate the impressions produced by external things. On this account the ancient kings were watchful in regard to the things by which the mind was affected.

So, they instituted ceremonies to direct men's aims aright; music

94

to give harmony to their voices;
laws to give integrity to their
conduct; and punishments to
guard against their tendencies to
evil. The end to which ceremonies, music, punishments, and
laws tend is one. They are the
instruments by which the minds
of people are corrected, and con-
tribute to good government.

The inner nature of man is the
province of music; that of ceremonies is his exterior. The result
of music is perfect harmony;
that of ceremonies the perfect
observance of propriety. When
one's inner man is harmonious,
and the outer man thus docile,
the people see it in his face, and
do not quarrel with him; they
look at his behaviour, and they
become neither rude nor indiffer-
ent. Hence the saying, "Carry
out perfectly ceremonies and
music, and give them their out-

ward manifestation and application, and there will be nothing under Heaven difficult to manage."

On Revenge

ZZE-HSIA asked Confucius how a son should act toward the man who has killed his father or mother. The Master said, "He should sleep on straw with his shield for a pillow; he should not take office; he must be determined not to live with the slayer under the same heaven. If he meet him in the market-place or in the court, he should not go back for his weapon, but fight him."

"Allow me to ask," said Zze-hsia, "how one should act if he has killed a brother." "He may take office," was the reply, "but not in the same State as the slayer; if he be sent on a mission by his ruler, though he may then meet the man, he may not fight him."

"And how should one do," continued Zze-hsia, "in the case of a man who has killed one of his paternal cousins?" Confucius said, "He should not take the lead. If he whom it chiefly concerns is able to do that, he should support him from behind, with his weapon in his hand."

On Riches

TO be full without overflowing
is the way to keep riches.

THE small man, when poor,
feels the pinch of his straitened
circumstances ; and when rich is
liable to become proud. Under
the pinch of poverty he may be
tempted to steal, and when become
haughty will be oppressive. The
rules of propriety take into consideration these feelings of men,
and lay down definite rules for
them. These serve as dykes for
mankind. Hence the sages dealt
with riches and honours so that
they should not have the power to
make men proud ; so that poverty
should not make them feel
pinched ; and that when in positions of honour men should not
be insubordinate to those above
them.

On Friendship

FAITHFULLY admonish your friend, and kindly try to lead him. If you find him intractable, stop. Do not disgrace yourself.

FRIENDS must frankly and sharply admonish each other, and brothers must be gentle toward one another.

WHEN a man on light grounds breaks off his friendship with the poor and mean, and only on great grounds with the rich and noble, his love of worth cannot be great, nor does his hatred of evil greatly appear. Though others may say that he is not influenced by love of gain, I do not believe them.

THERE was an old acquaintance of Confucius called Yuan Zang.

When his mother died, the Master
assisted him in preparing the outer
coffin. Yuan got up on the wood,
and said, " It is a long time since
I sang to anything," and began to
sing,—

" It is marked like a wild cat's head ;
  It is like a young lady's hand you hold."

CONFUCIUS, however, acted as if he
did not hear, and passed by him.
The disciples who were with him
said, "Can't you have done with
him ?" "I have heard," was the
reply, " that relations should not
forget their relationship, nor old
acquaintances their friendship."

On the Superior Man

THE superior man is rightly firm, not firm merely.

THE superior man thinks of virtue; the small man thinks of comfort.

THE superior man is catholic and not partisan; the mean man is a partisan and not catholic.

THE superior man is dignified but does not wrangle. He is sociable, but not clannish.

THE superior man is affable but not adulatory; the mean man is adulatory but not affable.

THE superior man has dignified ease without pride; the mean man has pride without dignified ease.

WHAT the superior man seeks is in himself. What the mean man seeks is in others.

THE superior man is distressed by his want of ability. He is not distressed by men's not knowing him.

TSZE-KUNG asked what constituted the superior man? The Master said, "He acts before he speaks, and afterwards speaks according to his actions."

THE superior man does not set his mind either for anything or against anything. What is right he will follow.

THE superior man is quiet and calm, waiting for the appointments of Heaven, while the mean man walks in dangerous paths, looking for lucky occurrences.

IN archery we have something like the way of the superior man.

When the archer misses the centre of the target, he turns around and looks for the cause of his failure in himself.

THE superior man bends his attention to what is radical. That being established, all right courses naturally follow. Filial piety and fraternal submission — are they not the root of all benevolent actions?

THE superior man takes no mistaken steps before men, nor errs in the expression of his countenance nor in the manner of his speech. Therefore his demeanour induces awe, his countenance induces fear, and his words inspire confidence.

THE superior man does not show his affection in his countenance, as if while cold in feeling, he could assume the appearances of affection. That belongs to the small man, and stamps him as not better than the thief, who makes a hole in the wall.

WHERE the solid qualities are in excess of the accomplishments, we have rusticity. Where the accomplishments are in excess of the solid qualities, we have the manners of a clerk. When the accomplishments and solid qualities are equally blended, we then have the man of complete virtue.

THE superior man in everything considers righteousness to be essential. He performs it according to the rules of propriety. He brings it forth in humility. He completes it with sincerity. This is indeed a superior man.

THE superior man does not confine himself to praising men with words ; and thus the people are loyal to him. When he asks about men who are suffering from cold, he clothes them ; or, men who are suffering from want, he feeds them ; and when he praises a man's good qualities, he goes further and confers rank on him.

Tsze-loo asked, "Does the superior man esteem valour?" The Master said, "The superior man holds righteousness to be of the highest importance. A man of rank, having valour without righteousness, will be guilty of insubordination ; one of the lower class, having valour without righteousness, will commit robbery."

I can find no fault in the character of Yu. He accustomed himself to coarse food and drink, but displayed the utmost filial piety towards the spirits. His ordinary garments were poor, but he displayed the greatest elegance in his sacrificial cap and apron. He lived in a mean low house, but expended all his strength on the ditches and water channels. I can find nothing like a flaw in Yu.

DOES he who knows the springs of things possess supernatural wisdom? The superior man, in his intercourse with them, uses no flattery; and in his intercourse with the low, uses no coarse freedom. Does not this show that he knows the springs of things? Those springs are the slight beginnings—the earliest indications of good fortune. The superior man sees them and acts accordingly without waiting for a single day.

HE who keeps danger in mind will rest safely in his seat; he who keeps ruin in mind will preserve his interests secure; he who sets the dangers of disorder before himself will maintain a state of order. Therefore the superior man, when resting in safety, does not forget that danger may come. When in a state of security, he does not forget the possibility of ruin. When all is orderly, he does not forget that disorder may come. Thus his person is not endangered, and his States and all their clans are preserved.

THE superior man composes himself before he moves others. He makes his mind restful and easy before he speaks. He settles his intercourse with others before he seeks anything of them. The superior man cultivates these three things, and thus needs nothing more. If he try to move others when he is himself disturbed, the people will not be influenced by him. If he speak while he is himself in a state of apprehension, the people will not respond to his desire. If without intercourse with them he issues his requests, the people will not grant them. When there are none in accord with him, his enemies will arise.

WHAT is termed making "the thoughts sincere" is allowing no self-deception ;—as when we hate a bad smell, and love what is beautiful, naturally and without constraint. Therefore the superior man must be watchful over himself when he is alone. There is no evil which the small man, living alone, will not do. But when he sees a superior man he tries to disguise himself, concealing his bad qualities and displaying his good. The other beholds him as if he saw his heart and mind. Of what use is his disguise ? This is an example of the proverb, " What is really within will be manifested without." Therefore the superior man must be watchful over himself when he is alone.

THE superior man has nine things which are with him subjects of thoughtful consideration. In regard to the use of his eyes, he is anxious to see clearly. In regard to his ears, he wishes to hear distinctly. As to his countenance, he is anxious that it should be benign. In regard to his demeanour, he is anxious that it be respectful. In regard to his speech, that it be sincere. In conducting business, he is anxious that it should be reverently careful. In regard to matters of doubt, he is anxious to question others. When he is angry, he thinks of the difficulties his anger may involve him in. When he sees he may acquire gain, he thinks of righteousness.

On the Superior Man

Long has the attainment of perfect humanity been difficult among men. It is only the superior man who is able to reach it. Therefore he does not distress men by requiring from them that which only himself can do, nor put them to shame because of what they cannot do. Hence the sage, in laying down rules of conduct, does not make himself the rule, but gives them his instructions so that they may be stimulated to endeavour, and shall be ashamed if they do not try to follow them. He enjoins the rules of ceremony to regulate conduct, good faith to bind it to them, right demeanour to set it off, costume to distinguish it, friendship to perfect it. He desires in this way to produce uniformity among the people.

It is only the sage that is possessed of that clear discrimination and high intelligence that fit him for

filling a high station, who pos-
sesses that enlarged liberality and
mild firmness that fit him for
bearing with others; who manifests that firmness and magnanimity that enable him to hold fast
to good principles; who is actu-
ated by that benevolence, justice,
propriety, and knowledge, that
command reverence; and who is
so deeply learned in polite learning and good principles, as to
qualify him rightly to discrimi-
nate. Vast and extensive are the
effects of his virtue. It is like
the deep and living stream that
flows unceasingly. It is substan-
tial and extensive as heaven,
and profound as the great abyss.
Wherever ships sail, or chariots
run; wherever the heavens over-
shadow or the earth sustains;
wherever the sun and moon shine,
or frost and dews fall, among all
who have blood and breath, there

is not one who does not honour
and love him.

THE superior man does what is proper
in the position which he is ; he
does not wish to go beyond it.
In a position of wealth and honour
he does what is fitting in a position of wealth and honour. In
poverty and meanness he does
what is proper in a position of
poverty and meanness. When
among barbarous tribes, he acts
accordingly. In sorrow or difficulty he does what is proper in
such a position. The superior
man can find himself in no position in which he is not himself.
In a high position he does not
insult or oppress those who are
below him. In a low position,
he does not cling to or depend on
those who are above him. He
makes himself right and seeks for
nothing from others. Above, he
does not murmur against Heaven ;

below, he does not find fault with men. He lives quietly and calmly, waiting for the will of Heaven, while the mean man does what is full of risk, looking out for turns of luck.

THE superior man stays at home and sends forth his words. If they be good they will be responded to at a distance of more than a thousand *li*. How much more response will they find in the narrower circle. He stays at home and sends forth his words. If they be evil they will rouse opposition at a distance of more than a thousand *li*. How much more will they rouse in the nearer circle? Words issue from the individual and affect the people. Actions come from what is near, and their effects are seen at a distance. Words and actions are the hinge and spring of the superior man. The movement of

that hinge and spring determine
glory or disgrace. His words
and actions move heaven and
earth. May he be careless in regard to them?

A RULER has only to be careful of what he likes and dislikes. What the ruler likes, his ministers will practise; and what superiors do, their inferiors will follow. This is the sentiment in the Book of Odes:

" To lead the people is very easy."

WHEN superiors are fond of showing their humanity, inferiors try to outstrip one another in their practice of it. Therefore those who preside over the people should cherish the clearest aims and give the most correct lessons, honouring the requirements of humanity by loving the people as their sons; then the people will use their utmost efforts to please their superiors.

ALL who have the government of the Empire with its States and families

have nine standard rules to follow: viz., the cultivation of their
own characters; the honouring of
men of virtue and talent; affection toward their relatives; respect toward the great ministers;
kind and considerate treatment
of the whole body of officers;
dealing with the mass of the people as children; encouraging the
coming of all classes of artisans;
indulgent treatment of men from
a distance; and the kindly cherishing of the princes of the
States.

Tsze-chang asked Confucius what
way a person in authority should
act in order to conduct government properly. The Master replied, "Let him honour the five
excellent, and banish the four bad
things; then he may conduct the
government properly." Tsze-
chang then asked, "What are the
five excellent things?" The

Master said, " When the person in authority is beneficent without great expenditure ; when he lays tasks on the people without their repining ; when he pursues what he desires without being covetous ; when he maintains a dignified ease without being proud ; when he is imposing without being fierce."

Tsze-chang then asked, " What are meant by the four bad things?" The Master said, " To put the people to death without having instructed them,—this is cruelty ; to require from them the full tale of work without having given them warning,—this is oppression ; to issue orders as if without urgency, and when the time comes to exact them with severity,— this is injury ; and, generally speaking, to reward men, yet do it stingily,—this is being a mere official."

FROM the loving example of one
family a whole State may become
loving, and from its courtesies,
courteous; while from the ambi-
tion and perverseness of the one
man the whole State may be
thrown into rebellious disorder.
Such is the nature of influence.
This is in accordance with the
saying, "Affairs may be ruined
by a single sentence; a State may
be quieted by one man."

Therefore the ruler must embody
good qualities in himself, and then
he may require them in others.
There never was a man who
could deal with others without
reference to his own character and
wishes. Thus we may infer how
"the government of the State
depends on the regulation of the
family."

Therefore the ruler must first be
careful about his own virtue.
Possessing virtue will give him

the people. Possessing the people will give him territory. Possessing the territory will give him wealth. Possessing the wealth, he will have resources for his expenditure.

Virtue is the root; wealth is its branches. If he makes the root his secondary object and the branches his first, he will only anger the people and teach them dishonesty. Hence the accumulation of wealth is the way to disintegrate the people, and the distribution of his wealth is the way to consolidate the people. In the same manner, when his words are not in accordance with that which is right, they will come back to him in the same way, and wealth got by improper means will leave him by the same road.

By the ruler's cultivation of his own character there is set up the example of the course which all should pursue ; by honouring of the worthy, he will be preserved from errors of judgment ; by showing affection toward his relatives, there will be no dissatisfaction among his uncles and brethren ; by respecting the great ministers, he will be kept free from mistakes ; by kindly treatment of the whole body of officers, they will be led to make the most grateful return for his courtesies ; by dealing with the mass of people as his children, they will be drawn to exhort one another to what is good ; by encouraging the coming of artisans, his revenue for expenditure will be sufficient ; by indulgent treatment of men from a distance, they will come to him from all quarters ; by his kindly cherishing of the princes of the States, all under Heaven will revere him.

THE princely man in dealing with others does not descend to anything low or improper. How unbending his valour! He stands in the middle, and leans not to either side. The princely man enters into no situation where he cannot be himself. If he holds a high position, he does not treat with contempt those below him; if he occupies an inferior station, he uses no mean arts to gain the favour of his superiors. He corrects himself and blames not others; he feels no dissatisfaction. On the one hand, he murmurs not at Heaven; nor, on the other, does he feel resentment toward man. Hence the superior man dwells at ease, entirely waiting the will of Heaven.

THE exercise of government depends on getting the proper men. Such men are to be got by the ruler's own character. That character must be cultivated by his adhering to a straight course. That course is marked out by benevolence. Benevolence is the chief element in humanity, and the greatest exercise of it is in the love of relatives. Righteousness is the agreement of actions with what is right, and the greatest exercise of it is in the honour paid to the worthy. The degrees of affection toward relatives and the steps of honour paid to the worthy are determined by the principles of propriety. When inferiors do not have the confidence of their superiors, the people cannot be governed well.

Therefore the wise ruler should not neglect the cultivation of his character. Desiring to cultivate his character, he should not neglect to serve his parents; desiring to serve his parents, he should not neglect to know men; desiring to know men, he should not neglect to know Heaven. The universal path for all under Heaven is fivefold, and the virtues by means of which it is trodden are three. These are, ruler and minister ; father and son ; husband and wife ; elder brother and younger ; and the intercourse of friend and friend. The duties belonging to these five relationships constitute the universal path for all.

Reflections

HAVE no friends not equal to yourself.

WHEN you have faults, do not fear to abandon them.

HOLD faithfulness and sincerity as first principles.

IT is characteristic of him who is entirely perfect that he can foreknow.

BY nature men are nearly alike ; by practice they get to be wide apart.

A SMALL man is drowned in the water ; a superior man is drowned or ruined by his mouth.

HE who acts with a constant view to his own advantage will not make friends.

TO have faults and not reform them —this indeed should be called having faults.

IF a man take no thought about what is distant, he will have sorrow close at hand.

I WILL not be afflicted at men's not knowing me; I will be afflicted at my not knowing men.

Sayings

WHAT is required in feeling is sincerity ; in words, that they be susceptible of proof.

A SAGE it is not mine to see ; could I see a man of real talent and virtue, I would be satisfied.

A GOOD man it is not mine to see ; could I see a man possessed of constancy, I would be satisfied.

THERE are only the wise of the highest class, and the stupid of the lowest class, who cannot be changed.

DISSATISFACTION and calamity will come to him whose lip-kindness is not accompanied by corresponding deeds.

HE who requires much from himself and little from others, will keep himself from being disliked.

THE commander of the forces of a large State may be carried off; but the will of even a common man cannot be taken from him.

THE mouth is talkative and troublesome; for words once uttered, there is hardly a place for repentance: men are easily ruined by the mouth.

FAN CH'E asked about benevolence. The Master said, "It is to love men." He asked about knowledge. The Master said, "It is to know men."

WHEN the multitude hate a man, it is necessary to examine into the case. When the multitude like a man, it is necessary to examine into the case.

THEY who know the truth are not equal to those who love it; and they who love it are not equal to those who delight in it.

WHEN we see men of worth we should think of equalling them; when we see men of the opposite character we should look inward and examine ourselves.

AT first my way with men was to hear their words and then give them credit for their conduct. Now my way is to hear their words and look at their conduct.

HE only is the sage who knows to go forward and to come back, to maintain and to let perish; and that without ever acting injudiciously. Yes; he only is the sage.

THE Path is not far from man. When men try to walk in a way that conscience does not approve, this course cannot be called the Path.

THOUGH a man have abilities as great as those of the Duke of Chow, yet is proud and niggardly, those

I

other things are not really worth looking at.

THINGS that are done it is needless to speak about. Things that have run their course it is needless to remonstrate about. Things that are past it is needless to blame.

WHEN a number of people are together for a whole day, without their conversation turning on righteousness, and when they are fond of carrying out the suggestions of petty shrewdness,—theirs is indeed a hard case.

THE meritorious services of Hay Ki were the greatest of all under Heaven. All that he desired was that his doings should be superior to his name, and therefore he said of himself that he was simply "a man useful to others."

THERE is a great course for the production of wealth. Let the producers be many, and the consumers few. Let there be activity in the production and economy in the expenditure. Then the wealth will be always sufficient.

How difficult it is to shoot! How difficult it is to listen to the music! To shout exactly in harmony with the note given by the music, and to shoot without missing the bull's-eye. It is only the archer of highest virtue who can do this. How can a man of inferior character hit the mark?

I KNOW why it is that the path of the mean is not walked in. The knowing go beyond it, and the stupid do not come up to it.

THERE is nobody but eats and drinks, but there are few who can distinguish flavours.

THERE was Shun. He indeed was greatly wise. Shun loved to question others, and to study their words, though they might be shallow. He concealed what was bad in them, and displayed what was good. He took hold of the two extremes, determined the mean, and employed it in his government of the people. It was by this he was Shun.

THINGS have their root and their completion. Affairs have their end and their beginning. To know what is first and what is last will lead near to what is taught in the Great Learning.

HE who knows how to show in himself what a son should be can afterward show in himself what a father should be. He who knows how to show in himself what a minister should be can afterward show in himself what a ruler should be. He who knows how to serve others can afterward employ them.

PLACES of burial should not be made to resemble pleasure-gardens. Rather they should be brought into harmony with those who weep and mourn. It was in this light that the ancients regarded them. To feast in luxurious apartments of the dead is an insult to their memory. More suited is some rugged height unfitted for the plough, where the pure and simple homage of the heart can be substituted for these vain frivolities.

The Progress of Civilization

IN the olden time, when Pâo-hsî had come to the rule of all under Heaven, looking up he contemplated the brilliant forms exhibited in the sky, and looking down he surveyed the patterns shown on the earth. He contemplated the ornamental appearances of birds and beasts and the suitabilities of the soil. Near at hand, in his own person, he found things for consideration, and the same at a distance, in things in general. On this he devised the eight trigrams, to show fully the attributes of the spirit-like and intelligent, and to classify the qualities of the myriads of things.

He invented the making of nets of various kinds by knitting strings, both for hunting and fishing.

On the death of Pâo-hsî there arose Shăn-năng. He fashioned wood to form the share, and bent wood to make the plough-handle. The advantages of ploughing and weeding were then taught to all under Heaven.

He caused markets to be held at midday, thus bringing together all the people, and assembling in one place all their wares. They made their exchanges and retired, every one having gotten what he wanted. They hollowed out trees to form canoes; they cut others long and thin to make oars. Thus arose the benefit of canoes and oars for the help of those who had no means of intercourse with others. They could now reach the most distant parts, and all under Heaven were benefited.

They used oxen and yoked horses, thus providing for the carriage of what was heavy and for distant journeys,—thereby benefiting all under the sky.

They made the double gates and the clapper, as a preparation against the approach of marauding visitors.

They cut wood and fashioned it into pestles ; they dug in the ground and formed mortars. Thus the myriads of the people received the benefit arising from the use of the pestle and the mortar.

They bent wood by means of string so as to form bows, and sharpened wood so as to make arrows. This gave the benefit of bows and arrows, and served to produce everywhere a feeling of awe.

In the highest antiquity they made their homes in caves, and dwelt in the open country. In subsequent ages, for these the sages substituted houses, with the ridge-beam above and the projecting roof below, as a provision against wind and rain.

When the ancients buried their dead they covered the body thickly with pieces of wood, having laid it in the open country. They raised no mound over it ; nor planted trees around ; nor had they any fixed period for mourning. In subsequent ages the sages substituted for these practices the inner and outer coffins.

In the highest antiquity government was carried on successfully by the use of knotted cords. In subsequent ages the sages substituted for these written characters and bonds. By means of these all the officers could be regulated, and all the people accurately examined.

In former times the public fields were cultivated by the united labours of the farmers around them, from the produce of whose private fields nothing was levied. A rent was charged for the stances in the market-places, but wares were not taxed. Travellers

were examined at the different passes,
but no duties were levied from them.
Into the forests and plains at the foot
of mountains the people went without hindrance, at the proper seasons.
None of the produce was levied from
the fields assigned to the younger
sons of a family, nor from the holy
fields. Only three days' labour was
required from the people in the
course of a year. Fields and resi-
dences in the hamlets could not be
sold. Ground set apart for graves
could not be bought.

The Minister of Works with his instruments measured the ground for
the settlements of the people. About
the hills and rivers, the oozy ground
and the meres, he determined the
periods of the four seasons. He
measured the distances of one spot
from another, and commenced his
operations in employing the labour
of the people. In all his employment of them, he imposed the tasks

of old men, and gave the food allowance of the able-bodied.

In settling the people, the ground was measured for the formation of towns, and then measured again in smaller portions for the allotments of the people. When the division of the ground, the cities, and the allotments were thus fixed in adaptation to one another, so that there was no ground unoccupied, and none of the people left to wander about idle, economical arrangements were made about food, and its proper business appointed for each season. Then the people had rest in their dwellings, did joyfully what they had to do, exhorted one another to labour, honoured their rulers, and loved their superiors. This having been secured, there ensued the institution of schools.

A Chinese Classic

THE name of Confucius was Yu, and his style Chung-ni; he established himself as an instructor in the western part of the kingdom of Lu. One day, followed by all his disciples, riding in a carriage, he went out to ramble, and on the road came across several children at their sports; among them was one who did not join in them. Confucius, stopping his carriage, asked him, saying, "Why is it that you alone do not play?" The lad replied, "All play is without any profit: one's clothes get torn, and they are not easily mended; above me, I disgrace my father and mother; below me, even to the lowest, there is fighting and altercation; so much toil and no reward, how can it be a good business? It is for these reasons that I do not play." Then dropping his head, he began making a city out of pieces of tile.

Confucius, reproving him, said, "Why do you not turn out for the carriage?" The boy replied, "From ancient times till now it has always been considered proper for a carriage to turn out for a city, and not for a city to turn out for a carriage." Confucius then stopped his vehicle in order to discourse of reason. He got out of the carriage, and asked him, "You are still young in years, how is it you are so quick?" The boy replied, saying, "A human being, at the age of three years, discriminates between his father and his mother; a hare, three days after it is born, runs over the ground and furrows of the fields; fish, three days after their birth, wander in rivers and lakes. What Heaven thus produces naturally, how can it be called brisk?"

Confucius added, "In what village and neighbourhood do you reside, what is your surname and name, and what your style?" The boy answered, "I live in a mean village and in an insignificant land; my surname is Hiang, my name is Toh, and I have yet no style."

Confucius rejoined, "I wish to have you come and ramble with me; what do you think of it?" The youth replied, "A stern father is at home, whom I am bound to serve; an affectionate mother is there, whom it is my duty to cherish; a worthy elder brother is at home, whom it is proper for me to obey, with a tender younger brother whom I must teach; and an intelligent teacher is there, from whom I am required to learn. How have I leisure to go a-rambling with you?"

Confucius said, "I have in my carriage thirty-two chessmen; what do you say to having a game together?" The lad answered, "If the emperor love gaming, the Empire will not be governed ; if the nobles love play, the government will be impeded ; if scholars love it, learning and investigation will be lost and thrown away ; if the lower classes are fond of gaming, they will utterly lose the support of their families ; if servants and slaves love to game, they will get a cudgelling ; if farmers love it, they miss the time for ploughing and sowing. For these reasons I shall not play with you.'

Confucius rejoined, " I wish to have you go with me, and fully equalize the Empire ; what do you think of this?" The lad replied, " The Empire cannot be equalized ; here are high hills, there are lakes and rivers ; either there are princes and nobles, or there are slaves and servants. If the high hills be levelled, the birds and beasts will have no resort ; if the rivers and lakes be filled up, the fishes and the turtles will have nowhere to go ; do away with kings and nobles, and the common people will have much dispute about right and wrong ; obliterate slaves and servants, and who will there be to serve the prince ? If the Empire be so vast and unsettled, how can it be equalized ?"

Confucius again asked, "Can you tell me, under the whole sky, what fire has no smoke, what water no fish ; what hill has no stones, what tree no branches ; what man has no wife, what woman no husband, what cow has no calf, what mare no colt ; what cock has no hen, what hen no cock ; what constitutes an excellent man, what an inferior man ; what is that which has not enough, and what that which has an overplus ; what city is without a market, and who is the man without a style ?"

The boy replied, "A glow-worm's fire has no smoke, and well-water no fish ; a mound of earth has no stones, and a rotten tree no branches ; genii have no wives, and fairies no husbands; earthen cows have no calves, nor wooden mares any colts; lonely cocks have no hens, and widowed hens no cocks; he who is worthy is an excellent man, and a fool is an inferior man; a winter's day is not long enough, and a summer's day is too long; the Imperial City has no market, and the little folks have no style."

Confucius inquiring, said, "Do you know what are the controlling bonds between Heaven and earth, and what is the beginning and ending of the dual powers; what is left, and what is right; what is out, and what is in; who is father, and who is mother; who is husband, and who is wife? Do you know where the wind comes from, and from whence the rain; from whence the clouds issue, and the dew arises; and for how many tens of thousands of miles the sky and earth go parallel?"

The youth answering, said, "Nine multiplied nine times make eighty-one, which is the controlling bond of Heaven and earth; eight multiplied by nine makes seventy-two, the beginning and end of the dual powers. Heaven is father, and earth is mother; the sun is husband, and the moon is wife; east is left, and west is right; without is out, and inside is in The winds come from Tsang-wu, and the rains proceed from wastes and wilds; the clouds issue from the hills, and the dew rises from the ground; sky and earth go parallel for ten thousand times ten thousand miles, and the four points of the compass have each their station."

Confucius asking, said, "Which do you say is the nearest relation, father and mother, or husband and wife?" The boy responded, "One's parents are near; husband and wife are not so near."

Confucius rejoined, "While husband and wife are alive they sleep under the same coverlet; when they are dead they lie in the same grave; how, then, can you say they are not near?" The boy replied, "A man without a wife is like a carriage without a wheel; if there be no wheel, another one is made, for he can doubtless get a new one; so, if one's wife die, he seeks again, for he also can obtain a new one. The daughter of a worthy family must certainly marry an honourable husband; a house having ten rooms always has a plate and a ridge-pole; three windows and six lattices do not give the light of a single door; the whole host of stars with all their sparkling brilliancy do not equal the splendour of the solitary moon: the affection of a father and mother—alas, if it be once lost!"

Confucius sighing, said, "How clever! how worthy!" The boy asking the sage, said, "You have just been giving me questions, which I have answered one by one; I now wish to seek information. Will the teacher, in one sentence, afford me some plain instruction? I shall be much gratified if my request be not rejected." He then said, "Why is it that mallards and ducks are able to swim; how is it that wild geese and cranes sing; and why are firs and pines green through the winter?" Confucius replied, "Mallards and ducks can swim because their feet are broad; wild geese and cranes can sing because they have long necks; firs and pines remain green throughout the winter because they have strong hearts." The youth rejoined, "Not so; fishes and turtles can swim. Is it because they have broad feet? Frogs and toads can sing. Is it because their necks are long? The green bamboo keeps fresh in winter. Is it on account of its strong heart?"

148

Again interrogating, he said, "How many stars are there altogether in the sky?" Confucius replied, "At this time inquire about the earth; how can we converse about the sky with certainty?" The boy said, "Then how many houses in all are there on the earth?" The sage answered, "Come now, speak about something that's before our eyes; why must you converse about Heaven and earth?" The lad resumed, "Well, speak about what's before our eyes— how many hairs are there in your eyebrows?"

Confucius smiled, but did not answer, and turning round to his disciples called them, and said, "This boy is to be feared; for it is easy to see that the subsequent man will not be like the child." He then got into his carriage and rode off.

Chinese Proverbs

NOT to distinguish properly between the beautiful and the ugly is like attaching a dog's tail to a squirrel's body.

AN avaricious man, who can never have enough, is as a serpent wishing to swallow an elephant.

WHILE one misfortune is going, to have another coming is like driving a tiger out of the front door while a wolf is entering the back.

THE tiger's cub cannot be caught without going into his den.

To paint a snake and add legs. (*Exaggeration.*)

To sketch a tiger and make it a dog is to imitate a work of genius and spoil it.

Chinese Proverbs

A FIERCE wolfish man is like the scathed branchless trunk of a tree.

To ride a fierce dog to catch a lame rabbit. (*Useless power over a contemptible enemy.*)

To attack a thousand tigers with ten men. (*To attempt a difficulty with incommensurate means.*)

To cut off a hen's head with a battle-axe. (*Unnecessary valour.*)

To cherish a bad man is like nourishing a tiger : if not well fed he will devour you ; or like rearing a hawk : if hungry he will stay by you, but fly away when fed.

HUMAN joys are like the skippings of a sparrow.

To instigate a villain to do wrong is like teaching a monkey to climb trees.

To catch a fish and throw away the net. (*Not to requite benefits.*)

151

To take a locust's shank for the shaft of a carriage. (*An inefficient person doing important work.*)

A PIGEON sneering at a roc. (*A mean man despising a prince.*)

To climb a tree to catch a fish is to talk much and get nothing.

To test one good horse by judging the portrait of another.

As a fish out of water so is a poor homeless man.

A FISH sports in the kettle, but his life will not be long.

LIKE a swallow building her nest on a hut is an anxious statesman.

LIKE a frog in a well is a man of small thoughts.

LIKE a crane among hens is a man of parts among fools.

LIKE a sheep dressed in a tiger's skin is a superficial scholar.

Chinese Proverbs

LIKE a cuckoo in a magpie's nest is one who enjoys another's labour.

To hang on the tail of a beautiful horse. (*To seek promotion.*)

Do not pull up your stockings in a melon-field, or arrange your hat under a peach-tree, lest people think you are stealing.

AN old man marrying a young wife is like a withered willow sprouting.

BY a long journey we know a horse's strength; so length of days shows a man's heart.

LET us get drunk to-day while we have wine; the sorrows of to-morrow may be borne to-morrow.

IF the blind lead the blind, they will both go to the pit.

GOOD iron is not used for nails, nor are soldiers made of good men.

A FAIR wind raises no storm.

The Wisdom of Confucius

A LITTLE impatience subverts great undertakings.

VAST chasms can be filled, but the heart of man is never satisfied.

THE body may be healed, but the mind is incurable.

WHEN the tree falls the monkeys flee.

THE tiger does not walk with the hind.

TROUBLE neglected becomes still more troublesome.

WOOD is not sold in the forest, nor fish at the pool.

HE who looks at the sun is dazzled, he who hears the thunder is deafened. (*Not to come too near the powerful.*)

HE desires to hide his tracks, and walks on the snow.

HE seeks the ass, and lo! he sits upon him.

154

An illiterate person is like a dry ink-stone.

Speak not of others, but convict yourself.

A man who has a tongue may go to Rome.

A man is not always known by his looks, nor is the sea measured by a bushel.

A gem is not polished without rubbing, nor is a man perfected without trials.

Ivory does not come from a rat's mouth.

If a chattering bird be not placed in the mouth, vexation will not sit between the eyebrows.

Prevention is better than cure.

For the Emperor to break the laws is one with the people's doing so.

Doubt and distraction are on earth, the brightness of truth in Heaven.

PUNISHMENT can oppose a barrier to open crime, laws cannot reach to secret offences.

WINE and good dinners make abundance of friends, but in time of adversity not one is to be found.

LET every man sweep the snow from before his own doors, and not trouble himself about the hoarfrost on his neighbour's tiles.

BETTER be upright with poverty than depraved with abundance. He whose virtue exceeds his talents is the good man; he whose talents exceed his virtues is the fool.

THOUGH a man may be utterly stupid, he is very perspicuous when reprehending the bad actions of others; though he may be very intelligent, he is dull enough when excusing his own faults; do you only correct yourselves on the same principle that you correct others, and excuse

156

others on the same principles you excuse yourselves.

IN making a candle we seek for light; in reading a book we seek for reason: light to illuminate a dark chamber, reason to enlighten men's hearts.

IF I do not debauch other men's wives my own will not be polluted.

BETTER not be than be nothing.

THE egg fights with the rock. (*Hopeless resistance.*)

ONE thread does not make a rope; one swallow does not make a summer.

To be fully fed and warmly clothed, and dwell at ease without learning, is little better than a bestial state.

A WOMAN in one house cannot eat the rice of two. (*A wise woman does not marry again.*)

The Wisdom of Confucius

THOUGH the sword be sharp, it will not wound the innocent.

SENSUALITY is the chief of sins, filial duty the best of acts.

PROSPERITY is a blessing to the good, but to the evil it is a curse.

INSTRUCTION pervades the heart of the wise, but cannot penetrate the ears of a fool.

THE straightest trees are first felled ; the cleanest wells first drunk up.

THE yielding tongue endures; the stubborn teeth perish.

OLD age is like a candle in the wind,— easily blown out.

THE blind have the best ears and the deaf the sharpest eyes.

THE horse's back is not so safe as the buffalo's. (*The politician is not so secure as the husbandman.*)

A WIFE should excel in four things—
    virtue, speech, person, and needle-
    work.

HE who is willing to inquire will
    excel, but the self-sufficient man
    will fail.

ANGER is like a little fire, which if
    not checked may burn down a
    lofty pile.

EVERY day cannot be a feast of
    lanterns.

Too much lenity multiplies crime.

IF you love your son, give him plenty
    of the cudgel ; if you hate him,
    cram him with dainties.

WHEN the mirror is highly polished
    the dust will not defile it ; when
    the heart is enlightened with wis-
    dom impure thoughts will not
    arise in it.

DO not consider any vice as trivial,
    and therefore practise it ; or any

Lionel Rogers
from
E. F. Railton.

Jan 1911.
"What is really within
will be manifested without" (p 109.)